- 2

F

Author:
Rupert Matthews was born in Surrey, England, in 1961. He was educated at his local Grammar School and has made a lifelong study of history. He has written over 150 books since becoming a full-time writer.

Artist:
David Antram was born in Brighton, England, in 1958. He studied at Eastbourne College of Art and then worked in advertising for fifteen years before becoming a full-time artist. He has illustrated many children's non-fiction books.

Series Creator:
David Salariya was born in Dundee, Scotland. He has illustrated a wide range of books and has created and designed many new series for publishers both in the UK and overseas. In 1989, he established The Salariya Book Company. He lives in Brighton with his wife, illustrator Shirley Willis, and their son Jonathan.

Editor:
Sophie Izod

Editorial Assistant:
Mark Williams

FIFE COUNCIL CENTRAL AREA	
792461	
PETERS	04-Sep-07
J935.03	£5.99
JPAS	RH

Published in Great Britain in 2007 by
Book House, an imprint of
The Salariya Book Company Ltd
25 Marlborough Place, Brighton BN1 1UB
www.salariya.com
www.book-house.co.uk

HB ISBN-13: 978-1-905638-10-9
PB ISBN-13: 978-1-905638-11-6

SALARIYA

1 3 5 7 9 8 6 4 2

A CIP catalogue record for this book is available from the British Library.

Printed and bound in China.
Printed on paper from sustainable sources.

Avoid being an Assyrian Soldier!

Written by
Rupert Matthews

Illustrated by
David Antram

Created and designed by
David Salariya

The Danger Zone

BOOK HOUSE

Contents

Introduction

Y ou are a farmer in Assyria during the reign of King Sargon II, in the year that will later be known as 720 BC. You live in the northern part of an area known as Mesopotamia. This means 'between two rivers', and includes all the lands around the Tigris and Euphrates rivers. To the north lie high mountains inhabited by strange tribes. To the south lies the dry desert. Your lands are rich and fertile, producing crops such as wheat, figs, plums, spinach and nuts. The rivers are filled with fish, and nearby forests have deer and other animals for you to hunt. Assyria is a rich and powerful kingdom that rules over nearby countries such as Syria, Israel, and even the mighty city of Babylon. Your ruler is King Sargon II, a wise and just king who enforces law and order. But other nations are jealous of Assyria. What keeps Assyria rich and powerful is its army, and you're about to discover that you really wouldn't want to be an Assyrian soldier!

Weapons you wouldn't want to be without!

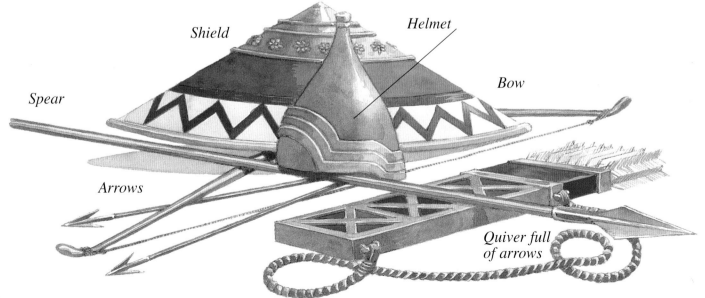

Shield

Helmet

Spear

Bow

Arrows

Quiver full of arrows

Your Turn!

Each year you have to hand over part of your crop to the government as taxation. You grumble because you don't always have a good harvest, but life is generally pretty good. You usually have enough to eat and you have your family around you. Each year government officials come to the village to decide who will have to go to work for the king. So far you have been lucky, and the officials have chosen somebody else. But this year you are really unlucky – you are called up to serve in the army!

Assyria was a country in the Middle East, covering parts of what are now Iraq, Turkey and Syria. The Assyrians conquered a vast empire – and it was the army that defended it.

ITALY

Please don't pick me.

Oink

What you'll miss:

A COMFORTABLE BED. Soldiers sleep on the ground, wrapped in a blanket. They have to get up early every morning to start work.

ROAST DUCK. Farmers have time to hunt local birds. But soldiers work all day, never get time off, and have to eat whatever rations they are given.

GIRLFRIEND. There are no women in the Assyrian army, and soldiers don't stay in one place long enough to meet anybody outside their regiment.

6

GREECE

Black Sea

TURKEY

Mediterranean Sea

SYRIA

ASSYRIA

IRAQ

Handy hint

You can get out of joining if you can get somebody else to go instead. If you are rich, pay a poorer man to take your place.

It's your turn!

Oh, no!

Grunnt

SAFE WORK. Ploughing may not be very exciting, but at least a plough never tried to kill you. Many people will try to kill you now that you are a soldier.

7

Heave!

The first few months in the army are very hard work. As a fresh recruit, you are forced to do all the jobs that the more experienced soldiers don't want to do. And there will be an officer with a whip watching to make sure that you don't slack. The Assyrian army needs roads on which to march and transport food, so your first job will be road building. You will chop down trees, shift boulders out of the way and carry heavy baskets of gravel to fill in holes.

BRIDGE BUILDING. The Tigris and Euphrates rivers that flow through Assyria, are among the widest in the world. You will help build and maintain bridges. Most bridges are made by inflating animal skins, tying them together and then laying a wooden road across the top. If you are given the job of rowing the skins out across the rivers, be careful not to fall off – especially if you can't swim.

Handy hint

All the worst jobs involve a shovel. If your officer is holding a shovel, stay out of his way in case he orders you to do a dirty job.

Ooh, my back! I hate shovels.

Dirty jobs

MAKING BRICKS. Assyrian bricks are made from sticky mud dried hard in the sun. You will get covered in mud.

LATRINES. Toilets are big holes in the ground that need to be emptied every few days. They will smell terrible.

DITCH DIGGING. Every camp is surrounded by a ditch as defence. You will get covered in dust and dirt.

FETCHING WATER. Large pots of water need to be carried to the camp every day. You'll probably get very wet.

Learn a Skill

After you have been in the army for a few weeks you will probably have grown a beard so that you look more like the officers. You will also be given the chance to learn a skill. Your officer will explain the opportunities to you. You may be told that a musician plays music instead of fighting, that a carpenter carves wood instead of digging ditches, that a cook stays away from the fighting, or that a servant just looks after an officer. But the officer is only telling you the good things about the jobs, not the bad things . . . so choose carefully.

Sounds too good to be true . . .

MUSICIAN. As a musician, you'll play music to help the troops march in step. This means you'll be first to get shot at. This is not a safe option.

CARPENTER. During battle, the wooden defences get damaged and it will be your job to mend them. The enemy will be trying to stop you repairing the defences. This is one of the most dangerous jobs.

COOK. There are thousands of men in the army who need feeding. You will have to peel tonnes of vegetables. This is very hard work indeed.

Handy hint

Learn how to write. Being a scribe is the best job in the army. You will not have to go into battle or do any hard work at all.

SERVANT. If your officer is injured, it is your job to to carry him off the battle field and avoid being injured yourself.

If only they knew . . .

Left, right! Left, right!

Y ou choose the infantry and are put into a group of ten men with a senior soldier in charge. Ten of these groups work together under the command of an officer. You will stay within this unit for the whole time that you spend as an infantry spearman. Your first task is learning to march. As a spearman you will be fighting in a tight formation of men. You will have to learn to march in step with the other men, how to turn at the same time as the others, and how to stop instantly. If you don't, you will get tangled up and trip over, your officer will shout and may punish you. If you get it wrong in a real battle it will be easy for the enemy to kill you. You must learn the basics quickly, or you will pay for it later.

Whoops!

OFFICERS. Your officer will stare at you a lot. He does not think you are pretty, he wants to be able to recognise you so he knows who he can order about.

STANDARDS. Your unit will have a special standard. You must learn to recognise it at a glance. In a battle you must stay with your standard and not get lost.

Ooof!

Now we'll be punished again!

Handy hint
Your shield is solid wood covered with a layer of bronze, and is very heavy. On long marches, use the strap inside the shield to sling it over your shoulder.

YOUR KIT. You will be given a water bottle, blanket, food pack and other kit. Look after it and don't lose anything, or you may be whipped.

HELMET CRESTS. Different types of soldier wear different crests on their helmets. Learn what the colours and shapes mean.

The King Speaks

When your training is finished, you take part in a grand parade in front of King Sargon himself! Your armour and weapons will need to be sparkling. You march up and down to show how well you have learned to follow commands. King Sargon then makes a speech about how important your role will be in the army, and what he expects from you. He tells you that King Pisiris of Carchemish has refused to pay the tribute he owes to the Assyrian Empire, and a war has begun. You must march to fight against Carchemish.

And you lot can attack first.

TURTAN. This is the most important officer in the army. If the king is not present, he commands the entire army. He carries a mace to show his rank.

RAB MUGI. These senior officers plan the campaign down to the last detail. They decide which route the army will take, and make sure there are enough weapons and food for everyone.

... for the glory of Assyria!

LUXURY. Unlike you, the king lives a life of luxury on campaign. He has tasty food served to him on beautiful plates. He can even bring his girlfriends along if he likes.

KNOW YOUR PLACE. If you take a message to a senior officer, bow down with your forehead on the ground to show proper respect.

The Siege of Carchemish

archemish is a large city surrounded by tall, strong defensive walls. In order to capture the city and punish King Pisiris, the Assyrian army will need to get inside these. Luckily, the Assyrian army is skilled at siege warfare. You are ordered to man a machine armed with two gigantic spears that are used to knock holes in the city walls. This first attack fails, so King Sargon orders the army to camp outside the walls, and wait until the people of Carchemish run out of food and surrender.

Siege warfare:
What you need to know

LADDERS. This is the quickest way to get into a city. But the defenders are waiting at the top of the ladder and they won't be very friendly.

TUNNELS. You could also dig a tunnel under the walls. Try to avoid this, though, since it's dirty, smelly, terribly uncomfortable – and dangerous too.

Handy hint

Sieges can last a very long time. Try to make sure you have a board game to make the days fly by.

Come on lads. A glorious death awaits you all!

Get in there and knock those walls down.

GATES. These are not as strong as the walls. Men with axes go forward to try to chop them down so that other soldiers can attack.

HUNGER. Those inside the city run short of food. If they get hungry enough, even rats start to look like a tasty meal.

Mmmm

Squeeaaak!

17

Grab it!

Looting is one way to get rich. After a battle, you get a certain amount of time to steal from the enemy. Carchemish is a large city full of people, so try to find out where the richest people live, and get there before any other Assyrian soldiers. You can take as much as you like, but try not to set fire to the buildings, and don't kill anyone unless your officer orders you to. King Sargon wants Carchemish to become part of the Assyrian Empire so it pays taxes to the royal treasury. Dead people and burned cities can't pay any taxes – and you really do not want to make King Sargon angry.

Pant

Wheeze

KEEP IT SAFE. Put your loot in a safe place so it cannot be stolen. Try sewing gold, silver or jewels into the lining of your coat so that you keep it with you at all times.

SELL IT. Merchants usually follow the army. If you manage to loot some furniture you could try selling it, but make sure you get a good price.

Hmmm

SEND IT HOME. You could send some home to your family to keep safe for you. Caravans of donkeys moved between the army and Assyria during the campaign.

SACRIFICE. Part of the loot has to be sacrificed to Asshur, the god of war. King Sargon will choose what to sacrifice, then throw it on a fire.

Shoot!

Nobody wants to stay a spearman all their life, so you volunteer to be an archer. You need to learn how to shoot a bow and arrow, but it will be worth it. You will be one of the most skilled men in the army and get special privileges. In battle, archers run ahead of the main army, trying to shoot arrows at the enemy army. You will be protected by a large straw shield called a 'gerrhon'. Even better, you don't have to carry it yourself – you get a servant to do that for you.

Twannggggg!

You are supposed to shoot at the enemy, not your own army!

GIVING ORDERS. As an archer, you have a recruit to carry your gerrhon around for you. At last you can give orders instead of just having to obey them all the time.

Arrrrgh!

Handy hint

A wet bowstring is useless, so keep it in a waterproof leather pouch.

Gasp

KEEP FIT. Archers need to be able to run quickly in battle so you're sent on long runs every day to make sure you're fit. If you fail, you will get kicked out.

ARROWS. You're given 40 arrows, and it's up to you to make sure that they are kept in good condition. Check regularly that they are straight.

THE FUTURE. A priest of the sun god Shamash pours oil into a bowl of water. With luck, Shamash will show you a vision of the future.

Battle of Musasir

our years after the siege of Carchemish, Assyria is invaded by the wild Urartu peoples from the northern mountains, led by their King Ursa. You are ordered north to stop the invasion. Near the town of Musasir, the Urartu set a trap for your army – and you march straight into it! A small force of chariots lures King Sargon II and the Assyrian chariots away from the main army. Then a powerful force of Urartu chariots attack you and the rest of the Assyrian infantry. You shoot your arrows as accurately as you can, but there are too many Urartu. Finally, you and your comrades run out of arrows. The Urartu charge, and your only chance is to run away.

CRASH! The larger heavy chariots are used to smash into formations of enemy infantry. The massive impact throws men in all directions as the chariots collide.

INSULTS. Lighter chariots are used to scout out enemy positions, then hurry back to tell Sargon the news. Many chariot crews take the opportunity to taunt the enemy soldiers.

QUICK GETAWAY. Most chariots are accompanied by spare horses. If the chariot crashes or overturns, the crew can escape on these horses. But the Urartu don't make it easy.

ROYAL CHARIOT. King Sargon II has his own personal chariot. It's decorated with plush fabrics and is very comfortable. A servant stands beside the king with a parasol, to keep the sun off the royal head.

Handy hint

A fast-moving heavy chariot is hard to stop or turn. If one comes towards you, get out of the way – fast!

Come back here!

The Assyrian chariots return at the last moment and defeat the Urartu. King Sargon realised that he had been tricked. He later claims that he had planned the battle this way all along . . . as if!

Chase to the Zab

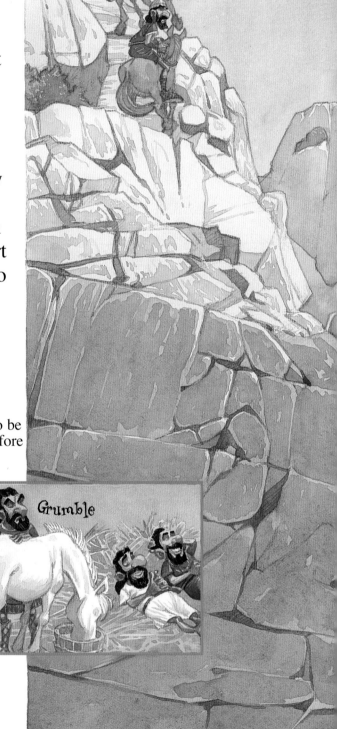

King Ursa escapes from the Battle of Musasir and flees north into the mountains. King Sargon orders your unit of archers to join a squadron of cavalry sent to hunt him down. You have never ridden a horse before, but there is little time to learn. You do your best to stay on the horse, and every night you are bruised black and blue. Eventually you catch up with King Ursa on the banks of the Zab River, and after a short fight, you capture him and drag him back to Assyria – King Sargon is delighted.

SHOVELLING MUCK. Horses produce a lot of droppings . . . guess who gets to clean it up.

GROOMING. Horses need to be fed, watered and groomed before you can rest yourself.

READY FOR ACTION. Tie the horse's reins to your hand while you sleep, or it will wander off.

Grumble

Handy hint

Archers must stand to shoot straight. Someone will have to hold the horses. Volunteer for this job as you will be safely out of the fighting.

After him!

LANCERS. Cavalry armed with long lances chase the Urartu. They prod bushes to find anyone trying to hide.

Ah-ha!

How do you make it stop?!?

Promotion!

After your success capturing King Ursa, you are promoted to join the Quradu – the most elite unit in the army. The Turtan himself welcomes you to this group, and there's more good news since you no longer need to grovel to other officers. As a Quradu, you will be given rich rewards, expensive new clothes and plenty of top quality food. But you are expected to be one of the best and most skilled soldiers in the army. You will also be sent on the most dangerous missions, and in battle you must protect the king at all costs. You will become rich and respected – if you survive.

Welcome to the best of the best!

SLAVE. You get a slave to do your cooking, washing, and polish your boots. For the first time since you joined the army, you don't have any chores to do.

REWARDS. On special occasions such as King Sargon's birthday, you can expect to be given gifts of gold jewellery, beautiful clothes and other rich treasure.

Handy hint

If you fight well you could get a rich reward – but only if an officer notices. Always make sure you can be seen clearly.

Glug

Glug

WATER FEATURE. You are expected to be expert at all military tasks – including swimming underwater using a goat skin full of air to breathe.

SPY. You will go ahead of the main army as a spy. Learn how to hide yourself well, because if you are caught, you will be executed instantly.

Going Home!

Many years after leaving, you return to your village. You are now rich and famous, as well as being a war hero. You bring your slave, and a donkey loaded down with treasures for yourself, and presents for all your family and friends. The village hasn't changed much, but you have! Everybody is pleased to see you – and some people are surprised that you have survived your time in the army. After all, you didn't want to be an Assyrian soldier!

Oinnnnnnk

SETTLING DOWN. Now that you are back home you can get married and settle down. It is time to find your old girlfriend and make up for lost time.

LOST ONES. While you were away several people have died – including your parents. Remember to visit the family shrine to pay your respects.

NEW HOME. With all the wealth you have gained from loot, and from serving in the Quradu, you are able to buy a large farm on which to live.

Handy hint

Write regularly while you are in the army to keep up to date with what is happening back home.

Oh, no!

Future Plans

RETIRED? As a former member of the Quradu you are a skilled and highly valued soldier. If the king is ever in serious trouble, or a major war breaks out, you may be called up to rejoin the army. You never know when the letter will arrive.

Sigh

EASY LIFE. As a rich man you can hire servants to work in your fields. You can stay at home and relax with your family instead of working hard.

Glossary

Archer A soldier skilled at using a bow and arrow.

Asshur The Assyrian war god, and patron of soldiers.

Assyria An area of the Middle East that now lies in Iraq, Syria and Turkey.

Babylon One of the richest and largest cities of the ancient world. The population of the city was close to a million at times. It stood near modern Baghdad in Iraq.

Carpenter A person skilled at working with wood, and able to build or repair all sorts of wooden objects.

Cavalry Soldiers who are trained to fight on horseback.

Chariot A wheeled vehicle pulled by horses that carries soldiers into battle.

Crest A decorative upright device made of feathers, hair or wool placed on top of helmets. The designs and colours identify different ranks of soldier.

Gerrhon A tall shield made of straw that is used by archers.

Infantry Soldiers who march and fight on foot.

Kit The various pieces of personal equipment given to each soldier.

Lancer A cavalry man equipped with a lance, a long wooden pole with a sharp metal spike on the end.

Latrine A temporary toilet used in army camps.

Mace A strong, heavy, wooden, metal-reinforced, or metal shaft, with a head made of stone, copper, bronze, iron or steel.

Mesopotamia The valley of the Tigris and Euphrates rivers. The word is Greek for 'between two rivers'.

Quradu The most important unit in the Assyrian army, made up of the best soldiers.

Rab Mugi Senior officers who specialise in organising supplies for the army.

Recruit Someone who is new to the army.

Sacrifice An offering made to the gods. Sacrifices were thought to keep the gods happy and win their support.

Scribe Someone able to read and write, whose job is to keep records and compile reports.

Shamash The Assyrian sun god, the most important of the gods.

Siege Military blockade on city, castle or fortified town.

Standard A symbol or object mounted on top of a pole that represents a military unit.

Taxation A payment made by people to their government.

Tribute A payment made by one country to another, usually to a larger and more powerful state.

Turtan The most senior officer in the Assyrian army.

31

Index